KU-127-617

Modernism in Russian Piano Music

Russian Music Studies

Malcolm Hamrick Brown, Founding Editor

Modernism in Russian Piano Music

Skriabin, Prokofiev, and Their Russian Contemporaries

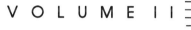

VOLUME II

Peter Deane Roberts

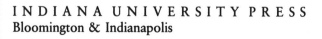

INDIANA UNIVERSITY PRESS
Bloomington & Indianapolis

© 1993 by Peter Deane Roberts

All rights reserved

No part of this book may be reproduced or utilized in any form or by
any means, electronic or mechanical, including photocopying and
recording, or by any information storage and retrieval system, without
permission in writing from the publisher. The Association of American
University Presses' Resolution on Permissions constitutes the only
exception to this prohibition.

The paper used in this publication meets the minimum requirements of
American National Standard for Information Sciences—Permanence of
Paper for Printed Library Materials, ANSI Z39.48-1984.

♾ ,TM

MANUFACTURED IN THE UNITED STATES OF AMERICA

Library of Congress Cataloging-in-Publication Data

Roberts, Peter Deane.
    Modernism in Russian piano music : Skriabin, Prokofiev, and their
Russian contemporaries / Peter Deane Roberts.
        p.   cm. — (Russian music studies)
    Includes bibliographical references and index.
    ISBN 0-253-34992-3
    1. Piano music—Soviet Union—20th century—History and criticism.
2. Scriabin, Alexandr Nikolayevich, 1872–1915. 3. Prokofiev,
Sergey, 1891–1953. I. Title. II. Series: Russian music studies
(Bloomington, Ind.)
ML734.R6   1992
786.2'0947—dc20   91-32124

1 2 3 4 5 97 96 95 94 93

CONTENTS OF VOLUME II

Acknowledgments

I am grateful to the publishers of the following works for permission to reproduce the excerpts so vital to the text:

Bridge: *Ecstasy* and *Bittersweet* (Ex. 14–1), Stainer and Bell.

Golyshchev: Trio (Ex. 13–14), by permission of the original publisher, Robert Lienau, Berlin.

Lopatnikov: Sonatine Op. 7 (Exx. 6–4, 7–2, 7–3, 9–29, 11–5, 11–8) and *Ironic Dances* (Ex. 6–7), Boosey and Hawkes.

Lourié: *Forms in the Air* (Exx. 7–18, 11–19), © by Breitkopf & Härtel, Wiesbaden; Nocturne (Exx. 5–22, 5–30) and Intermezzo (Ex. 5–27), Boosey and Hawkes.

Mosolov: *Nights in Turkestan* (Ex. 6–23) and Nocturne Op. 15 No. 2 (Ex. 6–34), reproduced by permission of Universal Edition A. G. Vienna.

Obukhov: *Berceuse of a Blessed* (Exx. 5–26, 9–20, 10–4), reproduced by permission of Editions Salabert, Paris/United Music Publishers Ltd.

Ornstein: *Dwarf's Suite* (Exx. 5–6, 5–10, 5–12, 5–16, 5–21, 13–1), *Wild Men's Dance* (Exx. 5–17, 5–18), Three Preludes Op. 20 (Exx. 13–2, 13–2), Schott and Co. Ltd.

Prokofiev: *Visions fugitives* (Exx. 4–3, 4–8, 4–11, 4–17, 4–22, 5–13, 5–14, 5–33, 6–10, 7–15, 7–17, 10–5, 10–12, 10–15, 10–16, 10–17, 11–14), Sonata No. 3 (Exx. 4–2, 4–16, 6–42), Sonata No. 4 (Ex. 4–13), Sonata No. 5 (Exx. 4–1, 4–4, 4–5, 4–7, 4–9, 4–12, 4–15, 4–18, 4–19, 4–20, 4–21, 4–22, 4–23, 4–24, 4–25, 4–26, 4–27, 4–35), and Rondo Op. 52 (Exx. 4–32, 4–33, 4–34, 4–36), Boosey and Hawkes; Toccata Op. 11 (Ex. 6–9), *Sarcasms* Op. 17 (Exx. 4–6, 4–10, 4–14, 4–28, 4–30, 4–31, 5–2, 6–11, 6–15, 7–1, 7–7, 7–xv, 9–14), and Sonata No. 2 (Exx. 4–14, 6–40, 9–13), Robert Forberg.

Roslavets: *Two Poems* (Exx. 3–11, 3–13, 6–2, 8–27, 8–28), reproduced by permission of Universal Edition A. G. Vienna.

Saminsky: *Folk Songs* Op. 28 (Exx. 10–6, 10–7, 10–8, 10–10), reproduced by permission of Universal Edition A. G. Vienna; and *Hebrew Songs and Dances* Op. 22 (Exx. 8–9, 9–11), Copyright © 1924 by Carl Fischer, Inc., New York. Copyright renewed. International copyright secured. All rights reserved. Reprinted by permission.

Shillinger: *Five Pieces* Op. 12 (Exx. 3–5, 3–6, 5–31, 5–34, 6–17, 6–37, 7–19, 8–2, 8–39, 10–2), © 1947 (renewed) by Associated Music Publishers, Inc. International copyright secured. Used by permission.

Skriabin: Prelude Op. 33 No. 4 (Ex. 2–4), Study Op. 42. No. 2 (Exx. 2–31, 8–22), and Preludes Op. 74 (Exx. 2–7, 2–12, 2–16, 2–19, 2–20, 2–21, 2–33, 2–34, 8–20, 8–35, 9–17, 9–25, 11–1, 11–4), Dover Publications, Inc.; Sonata No. 7 (Exx. 8–29, 13–xxxviii) and Sonata No. 8 (Ex. 2–15), International Music

Company; and "Fantasy Poem" Op. 45 (Ex. 2–14), Study Op. 49 No. 1 (Ex. 2–32), "Fragility" Op. 51 No. 1 (Exx. 2–3, 2–13), "Engima" Op. 52 No. 2 (Exx. 2–1, 8–23), "Desire" Op. 57 No. 1 (Ex. 2–2), Albumleaf Op. 58 (Exx. 2–5, 2–9, 8–24, 8–33), *Poem* Op. 59 No. 1 (Exx. 2–6, 2–10, 2–17, 2–18, 8–25), Prelude Op. 59 No. 2 (Exx. 2–11, 2–27, 2–i, 9–27), Poem Nocturne Op. 61 (Ex. 2–8), and "Etrangeté" Op. 63 No. 2 (Exx. 2–29, 2–30, 8–34, 9–21, 9–28), Peters Edition.

Shostakovich: *Three Dances* Op. 5 (Exx. 6–13, 7–9), Sonata Op. 12 (Exx. 6–1, 6–8, 11–3), and *Aphorisms* Op. 13 No. 6 (Ex. 5–29), Boosey and Hawkes.

Stanchinsky: Sonata (1911–12) (Ex. 6–14), Boosey and Hawkes.

Stravinsky: *Five Easy Pieces* No. 4 (Ex. 5–15), reproduced by permission © copyright in all countries 1919 J & W Chester Ltd., and *Three Easy Pieces* No. 1 (Ex. 5–23), reproduced by permission © copyright in all countries 1917 J & W Chester Ltd.

Tcherepnin, A.: Bagatelle Op. 5 No. 5 (Ex. 7–12), reproduced by permission of Heugel et Cie., Paris/United Music Publishers Ltd., *Pieces Without Title* (Exx. 5–9, 8–1, 8–31, 8–32, 8–38, 10–13, 10–14), © Durand S. A. Editions Musicales, Paris, avec l'aimable autorisation de l'Editeur; and *Sunny Day* Op. posth. (Ex. 10–11), Theodore Presser.

Modernism in Russian Piano Music

Musical Examples, Chapter 2

EXAMPLE 2-1. Skriabin: "Enigma" Op. 52 No. 2 (1906), bars 1–8.

EXAMPLE 2-2. Skriabin: "Desire" Op. 57 No. 1 (1907), bars 12–14.

EXAMPLE 2-3. Skriabin: "Fragility" Op. 51 No. 1 (1906), bars 1–4, 44.

EXAMPLE 2-4. Skriabin: Prelude Op. 33 No. 3 (1903).

EXAMPLE 2-5. Skriabin: Albumleaf Op. 58 (1910), bars 1–4, 8–10.

EXAMPLE 2-6. Skriabin: Poem Op. 59 No. 1 (1910), bars 1–2.

EXAMPLE 2-7. Skriabin: Prelude Op. 74 No. 5 (1914), bars 5–6.

EXAMPLE 2-8. Skriabin: Poem Nocturne Op. 61 (1911), bars 1, 23–24.

EXAMPLE 2-9. Skriabin: Albumleaf Op. 58, bars 17–23.

EXAMPLE 2-10. Skriabin: Poem Op. 59 No. 1, bars 1-2, 23-24, 36-39.

EXAMPLE 2-11. Skriabin: Prelude Op. 59 No. 2, bars 56–61.

EXAMPLE 2-12. Skriabin: Prelude Op. 74 No. 1, bars 2–4.

EXAMPLE 2-13. Skriabin: "Fragility" Op. 51 No. 1, bars 8–9.

EXAMPLE 2-14. Skriabin: Poem Op. 45 No. 2 (1904–1905), bars 13–16.

EXAMPLE 2-15. Skriabin: Sonata No. 8 Op. 66 (1913), bars 17–18.

EXAMPLE 2-16. Skriabin: Prelude Op. 74 No. 1, bar 1.

EXAMPLE 2-17. Skriabin: Poem Op. 59 No. 1, bars 9–13.

EXAMPLE 2-18. Skriabin: Poem Op. 59 No. 1, bars 25–26, 32–34.

EXAMPLE 2-19. Skriabin: Prelude Op. 74 No. 5, bar 8.

EXAMPLE 2-20. Skriabin: Prelude Op. 74 No. 3, bars 1–5.

EXAMPLE 2-21. Skriabin: Prelude Op. 74 No. 5, bars 14–15.

EXAMPLE 2-22. Musorgsky: "Eclipse" scene, *Boris Godunov.*

EXAMPLE 2-23. Musorgsky: Act 1 Scene 2 , *Boris Godunov.*

EXAMPLE 2-24. Wagner: *Tristan und Isolde*, extract.

EXAMPLE 2-25. Rimsky-Korsakov: *The Golden Cockerel.*

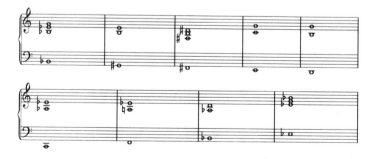

EXAMPLE 2-26. Rimsky-Korsakov: *The Snow Maiden.*

EXAMPLE 2-27. Skriabin: Prelude Op. 59 No. 2.

a. bars 1–3, 5, 54–55.

b. bars 11–13.

EXAMPLE 2-28. Skriabin: *Vers la flamme* Op. 72 (1914), reduction.

EXAMPLE 2-29. Skriabin: "Etrangeté" Op. 63 No. 2 (1911), bars 1–4.

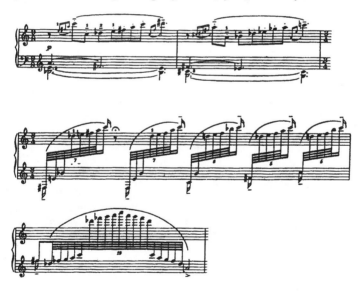

EXAMPLE 2-30. Skriabin: "Etrangeté" Op. 63 No. 2(1911), reduction.

EXAMPLE 2-31. Skriabin: Study Op. 42 No. 2 (1903), bars 1–4.

EXAMPLE 2-32. Skriabin: Study Op. 49 No. 1 (1905), bars 1–4.

EXAMPLE 2-33. Skriabin: Prelude Op. 74 No. 2, bars 1–4.

EXAMPLE 2-34. Skriabin: Prelude Op. 74 No. 4.

a. bars 1–8.

EX. 2-34b. bars 14–24.

c. scale of bars 1–8 and 17–24.

EXAMPLE 3-1. Vishnegradsky: Prelude Op. 2 No. 1 (1916), bars 1–2.

EXAMPLE 3-2. Vishnegradsky: Prelude Op. 2 No. 2.

a. bars 1–8.

EX. 3-2b. bars 17–18.

c. bars 25–29.

EXAMPLE 3-3. Shebalin: Sonata No. 2 Op. 7 (1927), second movement.

a. bars 29–30.

b. reduction.

EXAMPLE 3–4. Miaskovsky: Sonata No. 3 Op. 19 (1920).

a. bars 40–45.

b. bars 40–41, reduction.

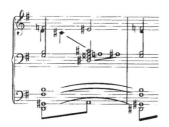

c. bar 46, transposed (reduction).

EXAMPLE 3-5. Shillinger: "Heroic Poem" Op. 12 No. I (1922).

a. bars 1–4.

b. bars 1–4, reduction.

EXAMPLE 3-6. Shillinger: "Heroic Poem" Op. 12 No. 1.

a. bars 41–52.

EX. 3-6b. reduction.

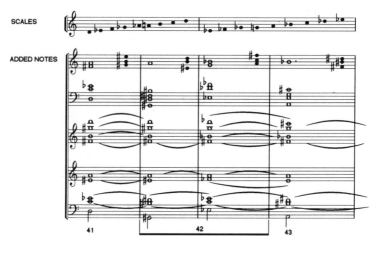

47 →

EXAMPLE 3-7. A. Krein: Sonata Op. 34 (1922), bars 1–11.

EXAMPLE 3-8. A. Krein: Sonata Op. 34, bars 12–46.

EX. 3-8 (cont.)

EXAMPLE 3-9. A. Krein: Sonata Op. 34, bars 47–56.

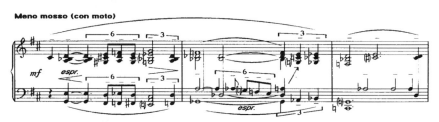

EX. 3-9 (cont.)

EXAMPLE 3–10. A. Krein: Sonata Op. 34, bars 99–104.

EXAMPLE 3-11. Roslavets: *Poem* No. 2 (1920).

a. bars 1–6, 18–27, 38–49.

Moderato; *sempre poco rubato.*

EX. 3-11a (cont.)

b. reduction.

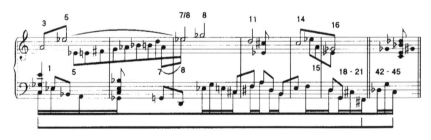

EXAMPLE 3-12. Roslavets: *Poem* No. 2, pitch chart.

		C	C#	D	D#	E	F	F#	G	G#	A	A#	B		
1	7	x	x			x		x	x	x		x		—	—
2	7	x		x			x	x	x	x		x		4	4
3	8	x	x			x		x	x	x	x	x		3	4
4	8			x	x	x	x	x	x		x	x		2	2
5	7			x	x	x	x			x		x	x	4	3
6	8			x	x	x		x	x		x	x	x	3	4
7	7	x	x			x		x	x	x		x		3	2
8	7			x	x		x		x	x		x	x	3	3
9	6	x		x	x			x		x	x			5	4
10	7			x	x		x		x	x		x	x	4	5
11	8			x		x	x	x	x	x	x	x		3	4
12	7			x	x	x		x	x	x		x		4	3
13	8	x		x		x	x	x		x		x	x	3	4
14	9			x	x	x	x	x	x	x	x		x	3	4
15	7	x	x	x		x		x	x			x		5	3
16	8	x	x		x	x	x		x		x	x		2	3
17	8	x		x	x		x	x		x	x	x		3	3
18	9	x	x	x	x		x	x	x		x		x	2	3
19	8	x		x		x	x		x	x		x	x	4	3
20	9	x		x	x	x	x	x		x	x		x	2	3
21	7	x		x	x			x		x	x		x	2	—
22	8		x	x	x	x	x			x	x		x	3	4
		13	15	14	13	14	14	14	15	17	12	14	13		

EXAMPLE 3-13. Roslavets: *Poem* No. 1 (1920).

a. bars 1–3, 16–18, 29–33.

EX. 3-13a (cont.)

b. reduction.

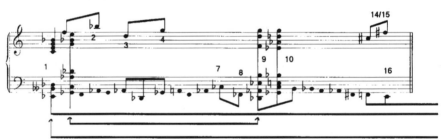

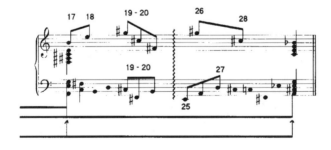

EXAMPLE 3-14. Roslavets: *Poem* No. 1, pitch chart.

a. bars 1–16.

		C	C#	D	D#	E	F	F#	G	G#	A	A#	B		
1	7		x		x	x		x	x		x		x	–	–
2	7	x	x	x		x		x	x			x		3	3
3	7		x		x			x	x		x	x	x	3	3
4	7	x		x		x		x	x		x	x		3	3
5	7		x	x	x		x			x	x		x	5	5
6	8		x	x	x		x	x	x	x	x			3	4
7	9	x	x	x	x		x	x	x		x		x	3	4
8	9	x		x	x	x	x		x	x		x	x	3	3
9	7	x	x				x		x	x	x	x		4	2
10	9	x	x		x	x	x		x	x	x	x		–	2
11	9	x	x	x	x		x	x		x	x	x		2	2
12	10		x	x	x		x	x	x	x	x	x	x	1	2
13	7		x	x			x		x	x	x		x	3	–
14	10		x	x		x	x	x	x	x	x	x	x	–	3
15	9		x	x		x	x	x		x	x	x	x	1	–
16	10		x	x	x	x		x	x	x	x	x	x	1	2
17	7		x	x		x	x		x		x	x		3	–
18	9	x	x	x		x	x		x	x	x		x	2	4
19	9	x	x	x		x	x	x	x		x	x		2	2
20	6	x	x		x		x		x			x		4	1
21	5		x		x	x			x	x				3	2
22	5	x			x	x			x		x			2	2
23	5		x		x	x			x	x		x		2	2
		11	20	15	10	15	16	13	19	13	18	16	12		

EX. 3-14b. bars 17–33.

		C	C♯	D	D♯	E	F	F♯	G	G♯	A	A♯	B		
1	7	x	x		x		x			x	x	x		–	–
2	7	x	x		x			x	x	x		x		3	3
3	7	x	x		x	x	x		x	x				3	3
4	7	x	x		x	x		x		x		x		3	3
5	7			x	x		x		x	x	x		x	5	5
6	7			x	x			x	x	x		x	x	2	2
7	8		x	x	x		x	x	x	x			x	1	2
8	9	x	x		x	x		x	x	x		x	x	2	3
9	7	x	x		x	x		x		x		x		2	–
10	7		x		x	x			x		x	x	x	3	3
11	6	x			x		x			x		x	x	3	2
12	7	x		x	x			x		x	x	x		3	4
13	8	x	x		x		x	x		x	x		x	2	3
14	7		x	x		x		x		x		x	x	4	3
15	10		x	x	x	x	x	x	x	x		x	x	–	3
16	10	x	x		x	x	x	x	x	x		x	x	1	1
17	8		x		x	x	x		x	x		x	x	2	–
18	9		x	x		x	x	x		x	x	x	x	2	3
19	9		x	x	x	x			x	x	x	x	x	2	2
20	9	x	x	x	x	x		x	x	x	x			2	2
21	9	x	x	x			x	x	x		x	x	x	2	2
22	8		x	x			x	x	x	x	x	x		3	2
23	7	x				x		x	x	x	x		x	4	3
24	8		x	x			x	x	x	x	x	x		3	4
25	7	x			x			x	x	x	x		x	4	3
26	7	x			x			x	x	x	x		x	–	–
27	7		x	x		x			x	x	x	x		5	5
		15	20	13	20	17	16	21	19	18	14	18	18		

EXAMPLE 3-15. Roslavets: *Three Compositions* No. 1 (1914).

a. score.

b. reduction.

EX. 3-15b (cont.)

c. harmony chart.

EXAMPLE 4-1. Prokofiev: Sonata No. 5 Op. 38 (1923), first movement.

a. bars 14–17.

b. reduction.

EXAMPLE 4-2. Prokofiev: Sonata No. 3 Op. 28 (1917), bars 52–61.

EXAMPLE 4-3. Prokofiev: *Visions fugitives* Op. 22 No. 1 (1917), bars 1–14.

EXAMPLE 4-4. Prokofiev: Sonata No. 5 Op. 38, first movement, bars 25–34.

EXAMPLE 4-5. Prokofiev: Sonata No. 5 Op. 38, third movement, bars 130–33.

EXAMPLE 4-6. Prokofiev: *Sarcasms* Op. 17 No. 2 (1913), bars 13–16.

EXAMPLE 4-7. Prokofiev: Sonata No. 5 Op. 38, third movement, bars 1–3.

EXAMPLE 4-8. Prokofiev: *Visions fugitives* Op. 22 No. 14 (1917), bars 1–2, 41–43.

EXAMPLE 4-9. Prokofiev: Sonata No. 5 Op. 38, first movement, bars 76–79.

EXAMPLE 4-10. Prokofiev: *Sarcasms* Op. 17 No. 1 (1912), bars 57–75.

EX. 4-10. (cont.)

EXAMPLE 4-11. Prokofiev: *Visions fugitives* Op. 22 No. 3 (1916), bars 1–4.

EXAMPLE 4-12. Prokofiev: Sonata No. 5 Op. 38, first movement, bars 1–8.

EXAMPLE 4-13. Prokofiev: Sonata No. 4 Op. 29 (1917), third movement, bars 255–59.

EXAMPLE 4-14. Prokofiev: Sonata No. 2 Op. 14 (1912), first movement, bars 103–20, reduction.

EXAMPLE 4-15. Prokofiev: Sonata No. 5 Op. 38, first movement, bars 12–16.

EXAMPLE 4-16. Prokofiev: Sonata No. 3 Op. 28, bars 19–27.

EX. 4-16. (cont.)

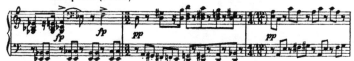

EXAMPLE 4-17. Prokofiev: *Visions fugitives* Op. 22 No. 12 (1916), bars 1–12.

EXAMPLE 4–18. Prokofiev: Sonata No. 5 Op. 38, second movement, bars 19–23.

EXAMPLE 4-19. Prokofiev: Sonata No. 5 Op. 38, first movement, bars 42–45.

EXAMPLE 4-20. Prokofiev: Sonata No. 5 Op. 38, first movement, bars 119–26.

EXAMPLE 4-21. Prokofiev: Sonata No. 5 Op. 38, third movement, bars 21–25.

EXAMPLE 4-22. Prokofiev.

a. *Visions fugitives* Op. 22 No. 11 (1917), bars 13–16.

b. Sonata No. 5 Op. 38, first movement, bars 56–63.

EX. 4-22c. Sonata No. 5 Op. 38, first movement, bars 72–76.

EXAMPLE 4-23. Prokofiev: Sonata No. 5 Op. 38, first movement, bars 198–200.

EXAMPLE 4-24. Prokofiev: Sonata No. 5 Op. 38, third movement, bars 13–19.

EXAMPLE 4-25. Prokofiev: Sonata No. 5 Op. 38, third movement, bars 58–73.

EXAMPLE 4-26. Prokofiev: Sonata No. 5 Op. 38, third movement, bars 32–41.

EXAMPLE 4-27. Prokofiev: Sonata No. 5 Op. 38, third movement, bars 105–12.

EXAMPLE 4-28. Prokofiev: *Sarcasms* Op. 17 No. 5 (1914), bars 17–20.

EXAMPLE 4-29. Prokofiev: **Abstract.**

EXAMPLE 4-30. Prokofiev: *Sarcasms* Op. 17 No. 1, bars 17–20.

EXAMPLE 4-31. Prokofiev: *Sarcasms* Op. 17 No. 1, bars 5-70, reduction.

EXAMPLE 4-32. Prokofiev: Rondo Op. 52 No. 2 (1928), bars 76–80.

EXAMPLE 4-33. Prokofiev: Rondo Op. 52 No. 2, bars 66–70.

EXAMPLE 4-34. Prokofiev: Rondo Op. 52 No. 2, bars 171–75.

EXAMPLE 4-35. Prokofiev: Sonata No. 5 Op. 38, first movement, bars 137–40.

EXAMPLE 4–36. Prokofiev: Rondo Op. 52 No. 2, bars 1–42.

EX. 4-36 (cont.)

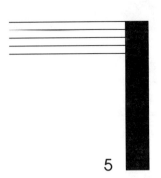

EXAMPLE 5-1. Shillinger: "Heroic Poem" Op. 12 No. 1, bars 1–9, reduction.

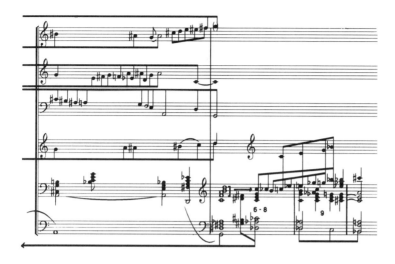

EXAMPLE 5-2. Prokofiev: *Sarcasms* Op. 17 No. 2 (1913).

a. bars 46–51.

b. reduction showing voice leading.

EXAMPLE 5-3. Feinberg: Sonata No. 5 Op. 10 (1921), bars 1–13.

EXAMPLE 5-4. A. Aleksandrov: Sonata No. 3 Op. 18 (c.1922), bars 17–23.

EXAMPLE 5-5. A. Aleksandrov: Sonata No. 6 Op. 26 (c.1924), second movement, bars 1–3.

EXAMPLE 5-6. Ornstein: "March Grotesque" Op. 11 No. 6 (1913), bars 40–43.

EXAMPLE 5-7. A. Aleksandrov: Sonata No. 3 Op. 18, bars 230–37.

EXAMPLE 5-8. Deshevov: *Meditations* Op. 3 No. 7 (c.1921), bars 1–5.

EXAMPLE 5-9. A. Tcherepnin: *Pieces Without Title* No. 5 (1914–18), bars 1–3.

EXAMPLE 5–10. Ornstein: "Funeral March of the Gnomes" Op. 11 No. 3, bars 1–14.

EXAMPLE 5-11. Shebalin: Sonata No. 2 Op. 7 (1927), second movement.

a. bars 1–15.

EX. 5-11a (cont.)

b. bars 18–25.

c. bars 40–41.

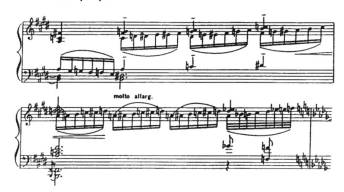

EXAMPLE 5-12. Ornstein: "Dance of the Dwarfs" Op. 11 No. 2.

a. bars 1–8.

EX. 5-12b. bars 84–88.

EXAMPLE 5-13. Prokofiev: *Visions fugitives* Op. 22 No. 4 (1917), bars 1–12.

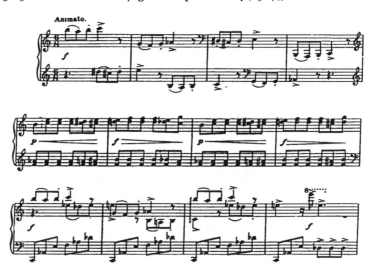

EXAMPLE 5-14. Prokofiev: *Visions fugitives* Op. 22 No. 2 (1916), bars 10–13.

EXAMPLE 5-15. Stravinsky: *5 Easy Pieces* No. 4 (1917), bars 1–7.

EXAMPLE 5-16. Ornstein: "Dance of the Dwarfs" Op. 11 No. 2.

a. bars 16–23.

b. bars 31–34.

EX. 5-16c. bars 36–37.

d. bars 38–43.

e. bars 44–47.

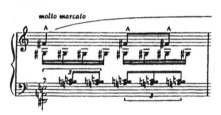

f. bars 53–57.

EXAMPLE 5-17. Ornstein: *Wild Men's Dance* Op. 13 No. 2 (1915).

a. bars 1–2.

b. bars 13–14.

c. bars 69, 73.

d. bar 90.

e. bar 109.

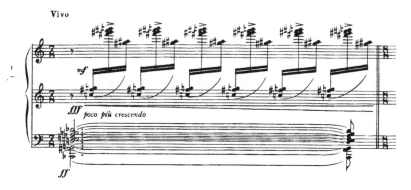

EX. 5-17f. bars 178–79.

EXAMPLE 5-18. Ornstein: *Wild Men's Dance* Op. 13 No. 2, bars 13–28.

EXAMPLE 5-19. Mosolov: Sonata No. 2 Op. 4 (1923–24), first movement.

a. bars 1–3.

b. bars 8–10.

EX. 5-19c. bars 34–36.

d. bars 40–42.

EXAMPLE 5-20. Mosolov: Sonata No. 2 Op. 4, first movement, bars 73–89.

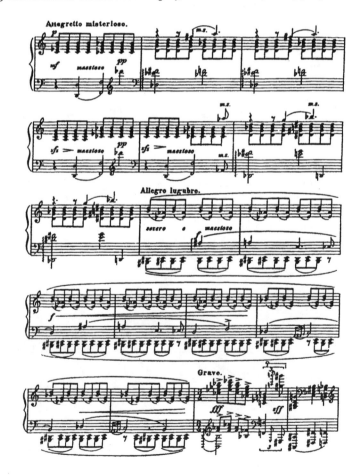

EXAMPLE 5-21. Ornstein: "Funeral March of the Gnomes" Op. 11 No. 3, bars 23–25.

EXAMPLE 5-22. Lourié: Nocturne (1928), bars 160–76.

EXAMPLE 5-23. Stravinsky: March from 3 *Easy Pieces* (1922), bars 5–8.

EXAMPLE 5-24. Feinberg: Prelude Op. 15 No. 3 (1922), reduction.

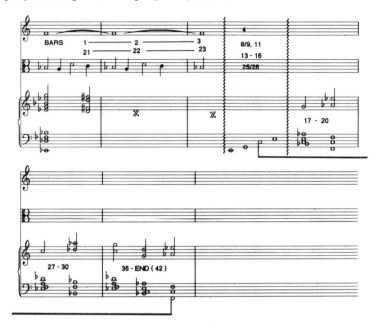

EXAMPLE 5-25. Deshevov: *Rails* Op. 16 (1927), bars 11–33.

EXAMPLE 5-26. Obukhov: *Berceuse of a Blessed* (1918).

a. bars 59–66.

EX. 5-26b. bars 71–83.

EXAMPLE 5-27. Lourié: Intermezzo (1928), bars 80–82.

EXAMPLE 5-28. Lourié: Sonatina No. 3 (1927), bars 1–4.

EXAMPLE 5-29. Shostakovich: *Aphorisms* Op. 13 No. 6 (1927), bars 13–25.

EXAMPLE 5-30. Lourié: Nocturne (1928), bars 1–23.

EXAMPLE 5-31. Shillinger: Dance Op. 12 No. 2, bars 1–21.

EXAMPLE 5-32. Lourié: *Syntheses* No. 2 (1914).

a. bars 1–7.

b. bars 16–26.

EX. 5-32b (cont.)

c. reduction.

EXAMPLE 5-33. Prokofiev: *Visions fugitives* Op. 22 No. 6 (1915), bars 1–19.

EXAMPLE 5-34. Shillinger: "Grotesque" Op. 12 No. 5.

a. bars 1–9.

EX. 5-34b. bar 71.

c. bars 105–107.

EXAMPLE 6-1. Shostakovich: Sonata Op. 12 (1926), bars 46–62.

EXAMPLE 6-2. Roslavets: Sonata for Violin and Piano (1913), bars 49–50.

EXAMPLE 6-3. Mosolov: Sonata No. 2 Op. 4, first movement, bars 67–72.

EXAMPLE 6-4. Lopatnikov: Sonatina Op. 7 (1928), second movement, bars 3–15.

EXAMPLE 6-5. Feinberg: Sonata No. 5 Op. 10, bars 37–39.

EXAMPLE 6-6. A. Tcherepnin: Dance Op. 2 No. 2 (1919), bars 1–39.

Piano.

EX. 6-6 (cont.)

EXAMPLE 6-7. Lopatnikov: *Ironic Dances* Op. 13 No. 2 (1929), bars 17–24.

EXAMPLE 6-8. Shostakovich: Sonata Op. 12.

a. bars 112–19.

b. bars 188–96.

EX. 6-8c. bars 228–38.

d. bars 1–2.

e. bars 37–42.

EXAMPLE 6-9. Prokofiev: Toccata Op. 11 (1912), bars 175–80.

EXAMPLE 6-10. Prokofiev: *Visions fugitives* Op. 22 No. 8 (1917), bars 1–3.

EXAMPLE 6-11. Prokofiev: *Sarcasms* Op. 17 No. 5, bars 57–67.

EXAMPLE 6-12. Lourié: *Syntheses* No. 5, bars 1–14.

EXAMPLE 6-13. Shostakovich: *Three Fantastic Dances* Op. 5 No. 1 (1925), bars 1–13.

EXAMPLE 6-14. Stanchinsky: Sonata (1911–12), bars 108–11.

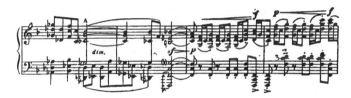

EXAMPLE 6-15. Prokofiev: *Sarcasms* Op. 17 No. 2, bars 21–29.

EXAMPLE 6-16. Deshevov: *Rails* Op. 16, bars 50–57.

EXAMPLE 6-17. Shillinger: "Grotesque" Op. 12 No. 5, bars 31–58.

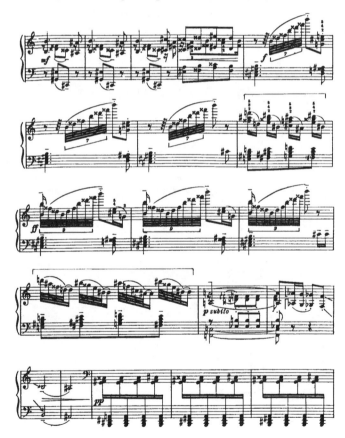

EXAMPLE 6-18. Liatoshinsky: Sonata No. 2 Op. 18 (1925), bars 121–26.

EXAMPLE 6-19. A. Aleksandrov: Sonata No. 6 Op. 26, first movement, bars 115–17.

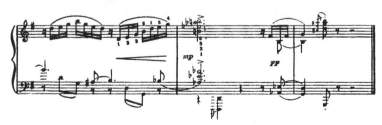

EXAMPLE 6-20. Deshevov: *Meditations* Op. 3 No. 4, bars 21–33.

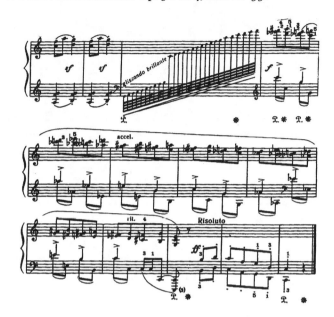

EXAMPLE 6-21. A. Krein: Op. 18 No. 2 (c.1918), bars 39–48.

EXAMPLE 6-22. Mosolov: Sonata No. 2 Op. 4, first movement, bars 162–72.

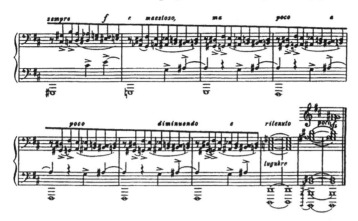

EXAMPLE 6-23. Mosolov: *Nights in Turkestan* No. 2 (1928), bars 59–66.

EXAMPLE 6-24. G. Krein: Sonata Op. 27 (1925), bars 703–709.

EX. 6-24 (cont.)

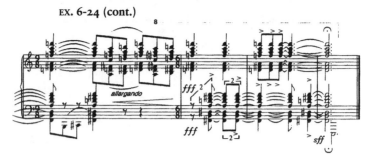

EXAMPLE 6-25. Liatoshinsky: Sonata No. 1 Op. 13 (1924), bars 172–74.

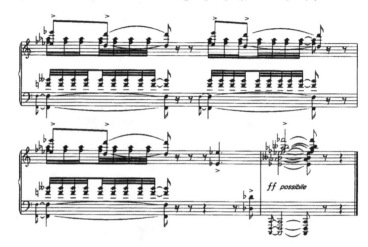

EXAMPLE 6-26. A. Aleksandrov: Sonata No. 6 Op. 26, third movement, bars 48–54.

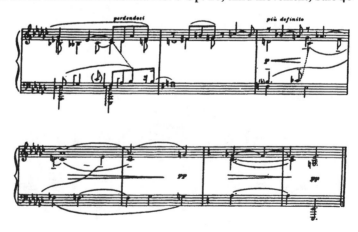

EXAMPLE 6-27. Kriukov: *Schlaflose Nacht* Op. 12 (1923), bars 71–79.

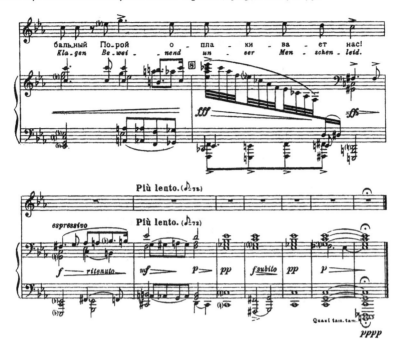

EXAMPLE 6-28. A. Aleksandrov: Sonata No. 6 Op. 26, third movement, bars 118–23.

EXAMPLE 6-29. A. Aleksandrov: Sonata No. 3 Op. 18, bars 349–52.

EXAMPLE 6-30. Miaskovsky: Sonata No. 3 Op. 19 (1920), bars 200–204.

EXAMPLE 6-31. A. Krein: Sonata Op. 34 (1922), bars 257–67.

EXAMPLE 6-32. Sabaneev: Sonata Op. 15 (1915), bars 558–83.

EX. 6-32 (cont.)

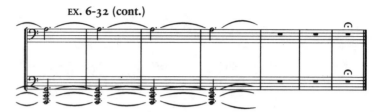

EXAMPLE 6-33. Mosolov: Sonata No. 2 Op. 4, third movement, bars 164–69.

EXAMPLE 6-34. Mosolov: Nocturne Op. 15 No. 2 (1926), bars 20–22.

EXAMPLE 6-35. Kriukov: Sonata No. 2 Op. 14 (1922–24), bars 335–51.

EXAMPLE 6-36. Lourié: *Upmann Smoking Sketch* (1917), bars 20–22.

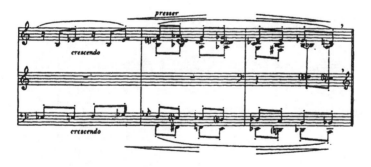

EXAMPLE 6-37. Shillinger: "Eccentric Dance" Op. 12 No. 4, bars 1–15.

EXAMPLE 6-38. Miaskovsky: Sonata No. 3 Op. 19, bars 1–11.

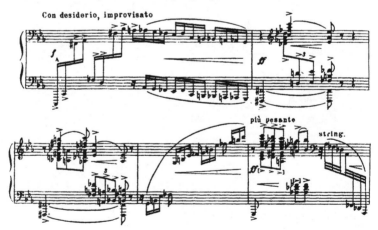

EXAMPLE 6-39. Lourié: *Syntheses* No. 1, bars 1–2.

EXAMPLE 6-40. Prokofiev: Sonata No. 2 Op. 14, third movement, bars 177–94.

EXAMPLE 6-41. Shebalin: Sonata No. 2 Op. 7, first movement, bars 28–36.

EXAMPLE 6-42. Prokofiev: Sonata No. 3 Op. 28, bars 1–7.

EXAMPLE 6-43. Roslavets: Poem (1916).

a. bars 1–24.

EX. 6-43a (cont.)

b. reduction.

EXAMPLE 6-44. Mosolov: Sonata No. 2 Op. 4, first movement.

a. bars 43–66.

EX. 6-44b. reduction.

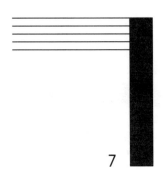

EXAMPLE 7-1. Prokofiev: *Sarcasms* Op. 17 No. 2, bars 1–12.

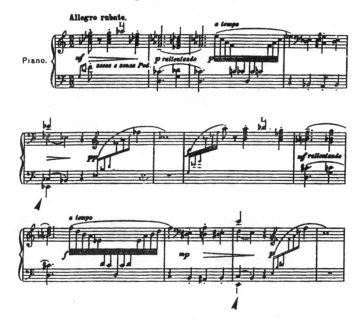

EXAMPLE 7-2. Lopatnikov: Sonatina Op. 7, first movement.

a. bars 1–4.

EX. 7-2b. bars 11–12.

c. bars 19–20.

d. bars 33–34.

e. bars 57–62.

EXAMPLE 7-3. Lopatnikov: Sonatina Op. 7, third movement.

a. bars 1–3.

b. bars 44–59.

c. bars 80–83.

d. bars 92–104.

EX. 7-3d (cont.)

e. bars 209–16.

EXAMPLE 7-4. Shebalin: Sonata No. 2 Op. 7, first movement.

a. bars 1–10.

b. bars 198–208.

EXAMPLE 7-5. Shaporin: Scherzo Op. 5a (1924), bars 179–92.

EXAMPLE 7-6. Deshevov: *Meditations* Op. 3 No. 3.

a. bars 1–12.

b. bars 16–30.

EXAMPLE 7-7. Prokofiev: *Sarcasms* Op. 17 No. 1, bars 117–26.

EXAMPLE 7-8. Mosolov: Sonata No. 1 Op. 3 (1924), bars 38–59.

EXAMPLE 7-9. Shostakovich: Three Fantastic Dances Op. 5 No. 3.

a. bars 1–13.

b. bars 34–42.

EXAMPLE 7–10. Miaskovsky: Sonata No. 3 Op. 19.

a. bars 6–8.

b. bars 25–27.

EXAMPLE 7-11. Deshevov: *Meditations* Op. 3 No. 6.

EXAMPLE 7-12. A. Tcherepnin: Bagatelle Op. 5 No. 5 (1923).

EXAMPLE 7-13. Feinberg: Sonata No. 5 Op. 10.

a. bars 44–57.

EX. 7-13a (cont.)

b. bars 146–58.

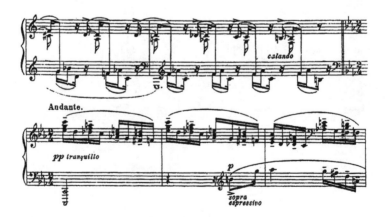

c. reduction.

EXAMPLE 7-14. A. Aleksandrov: Sonata No. 3 Op. 18.

a. reduction.

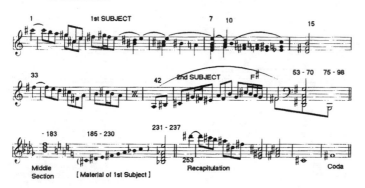

EX. 7-14b. bars 123–41.

EXAMPLE 7-15. Prokofiev: *Visions fugitives* Op. 22 No. 18 (1917), bars 21–32.

EXAMPLE 7-16. A. Krein: Sonata Op. 34, bars 85–90.

EXAMPLE 7-17. Prokofiev: *Visions fugitives* Op. 22 No. 19 (1917).

a. bars 1–13.

EX. 7-17b. bars 29–40.

EXAMPLE 7–18. Lourié: *Forms in the Air* (1915), first movement, cell 1.

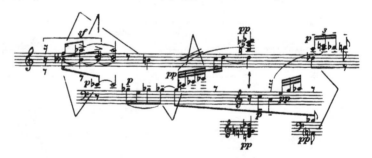

EXAMPLE 7-19. Shillinger: "Heroic Poem" Op. 12 No. 1, bars 56–60.

EXAMPLE 7-20. A. Aleksandrov: Sonata No. 3 Op. 18, bars 326–39.

EXAMPLE 7-21. Mosolov: Sonata No. 2 Op. 4, first movement, bars 24–36.

EX. 7-21 (cont.)

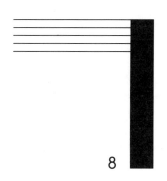

EXAMPLE 8-1. A. Tcherepnin: *Pieces Without Title* No. 3, bars 1–6.

EXAMPLE 8-2. Shillinger: Dance Op. 12 No. 2, bars 25–29.

EXAMPLE 8-3. Folk song from the Pechora region of Russia.

EXAMPLE 8-4. Abstract of folk scale.

EXAMPLE 8-5. Folk song from Moldavia.

EXAMPLE 8-6. Music of the Bashkir people.

a. folk song from the Ural region.

b. reduction of Example 8-6a.

c. analysis of a Bashkir folk song.

EXAMPLE 8-7. **Folk song of the Buryat-Mongol people of Siberia.**

a. score.

EX. 8-7b. reduction.

EXAMPLE 8-8. "Deli Yaman," folk song from Armenia.

a. score.

b. scale.

EXAMPLE 8-9. Sabbath dance in a setting by Saminsky, Op. 22 No. 7.

a. bars 17–24.

b. scale.

EXAMPLE 8-10. Rimsky-Korsakov: *The Golden Cockerel.*

EXAMPLE 8-11. Rimsky-Korsakov: *The Golden Cockerel.*

EXAMPLE 8-12. Rimsky-Korsakov: *The Golden Cockerel.*

EXAMPLE 8-13. Rimsky-Korsakov: *The Golden Cockerel.*

EXAMPLE 8-14. Rimsky-Korsakov: *The Golden Cockerel.*

EXAMPLE 8-15. Rimsky-Korsakov: Bird song from *The Snow Maiden.*

EXAMPLE 8-16. Glinka: *Ruslan and Liudmila.*

EXAMPLE 8-17. Musorgsky: *Boris Godunov.*

EXAMPLE 8-18. Protopopov: Chart from *The Elements of Musical Speech.*

EXAMPLE **8-19.** Russian folk song "Prialitsa."

EXAMPLE **8-20.** Skriabin: Prelude Op. 74 No. 5.

a. bars 1–3.

b. bars 5–8.

EXAMPLE 8-21. Musorgsky: Clock scene from *Boris Godunov*.

EXAMPLE 8-22. Skriabin: Study Op. 42 No. 2, bars 1–3, 7–9.

EXAMPLE 8–23. Skriabin: "Enigma" Op. 52 No. 2.

a. bars 1–22.

b. bars 29–46.

EXAMPLE 8-24. Skriabin: Albumleaf Op. 58, extract.

BARS 3 - 5   7 - 11   20 - 21   2 ·6 ·17

EXAMPLE 8-25. Skriabin: Poem Op. 59 No. 1, extract.

EXAMPLE 8-26. Roslavets: Poem No. 1 (1920), extract.

EXAMPLE 8-27. Roslavets: Poem No. 2 (1920), bars 7–12.

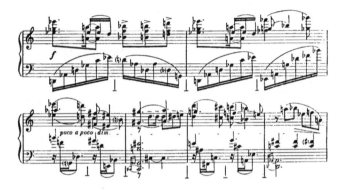

EXAMPLE 8-28. Roslavets: Poem No. 1 (1920), bars 1–3, 9–10.

EXAMPLE 8-29. Skriabin: Sonata No. 7 Op. 64 (1911), bars 177–82.

EXAMPLE 8-30. Folk song from the Don River region of Russia.

EXAMPLE 8-31. A. Tcherepnin: *Pieces Without Title* No. 7.

a. bars 7–14.

b. reduction, bars 9–10.

EX. 8-31c. reduction, bar 11.

EXAMPLE 8-32. A. Tcherepnin: *Pieces Without Title* No. 8, bars 4–15.

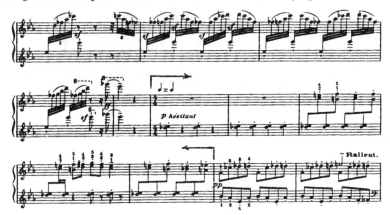

EXAMPLE 8-33. Skriabin: Albumleaf Op. 58.

a. bars 5–18.

b. reduction.

c. reduction.

EXAMPLE 8-34. Skriabin: "Etrangeté" Op. 63 No. 2, extracts.

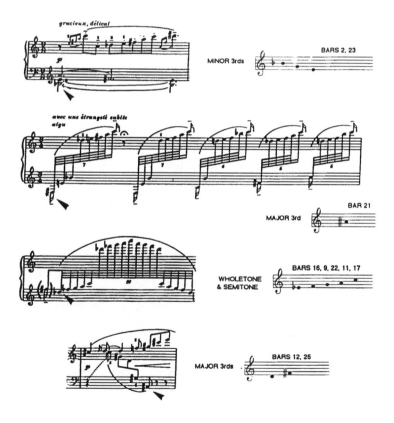

EX. 8-34 (cont.)

EXAMPLE 8-35. Skriabin: Prelude Op. 74 No. 1.

a. bars 1–16.

b. reduction.

c. reduction.

END OF BAR 5-6   END OF BAR 7-8

EXAMPLE 8-36. Skriabin: Sonata No. 10 Op. 70 (1913).

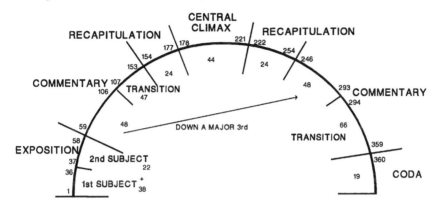

EXAMPLE 8-37. A. Krein: Sonata Op. 34, bars 1–16, reduction.

EX. 8-37 (cont.)

EXAMPLE 8-38. A. Tcherepnin: *Pieces Without Title* No. 5.

a. bars 1–7.

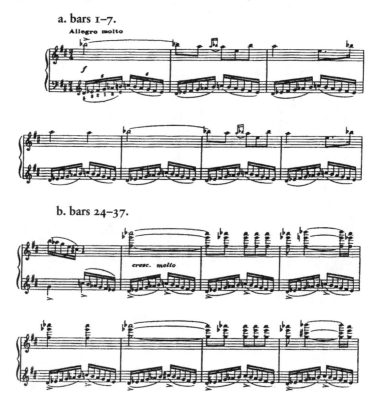

b. bars 24–37.

EXAMPLE 8-39. Shillinger: "Humming Machines" Op. 12 No. 3.

a. bars 1–10.

EX. 8-39b. reduction.

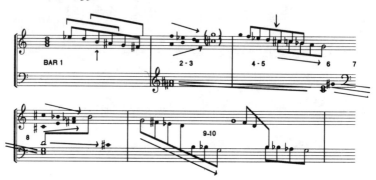

EXAMPLE 9-1. Dargomyzhsky: *The Stone Guest.*

EXAMPLE 9-2. Musorgsky: "The Cockchafer."

EXAMPLE 9-3. Rimsky-Korsakov: *Sadko* (1894–96).

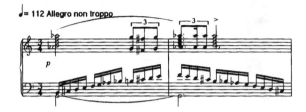

EXAMPLE 9-4. Rimsky-Korsakov: *Sadko* Op. 5 (1869).

EXAMPLE 9-5. Rimsky-Korsakov: *The Snow Maiden.*

EXAMPLE 9-6. Rimsky-Korsakov: *Antar* Symphony.

EXAMPLE 9-7. Scales of Russian work cries.

EXAMPLE 9-8. Two folk songs from the Pechora region of Russia.

EXAMPLE 9-9. Folk song from Armenia.

EXAMPLE 9-10. "Song of the Homeless," Armenian folk song.

EXAMPLE 9-11. Russian Hebrew dance in a setting by Saminsky, Op. 22 No. 10.

EXAMPLE 9-12. **Folk song from Armenia.**

EXAMPLE 9-13. **Prokofiev: Sonata No. 2 Op. 14, third movement, bars 213–23.**

EXAMPLE 9-14. **Prokofiev: *Sarcasms* Op. 17 No. 4 (1914), bars 1–4.**

EXAMPLE 9-15. A. Tcherepnin: Toccata Op. 1 (1921).

a. bars 28–44.

b. bars 90–108.

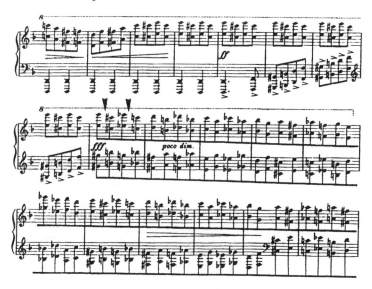

EXAMPLE 9-16. Vishnegradsky: *Autumn* Op. 1 (1917), bars 63–69.

EXAMPLE 9-17. Scale from Skriabin's Prelude Op. 74 No. 4.

EXAMPLE 9-18. Scale from a Chasidic dance in a setting by Saminsky, Op. 22 No. 4.

EXAMPLE 9-19. A. Krein: Sonata Op. 34, bars 91–94.

EXAMPLE 9-20. Obukhov: *Berceuse of a Blessed*, bars 28–34.

EXAMPLE 9-21. Skriabin: "Etrangeté" Op. 63 No. 2, bars 12–16.

EXAMPLE 9-22. A. Krein: Sonata Op. 34, reduction.

EXAMPLE 9-23. A. Krein: Sonata Op. 34, bars 55–68.

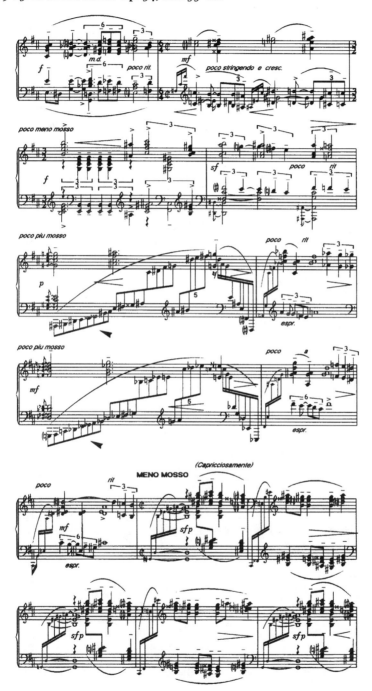

EXAMPLE 9-24. A. Aleksandrov: Sonata No. 3 Op. 18.

a. bars 55–59.

b. bars 65–66.

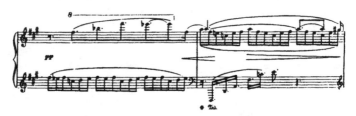

c. bars 75–76.

d. bars 208–11.

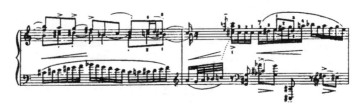

EXAMPLE 9-25. Skriabin: Op. 74, scale chart.

EX. 9-25 (cont.)

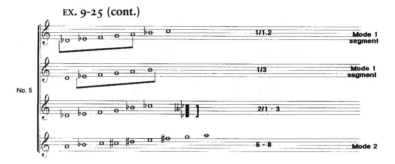

EXAMPLE 9-26. Roslavets: Poem (1916), reduction.

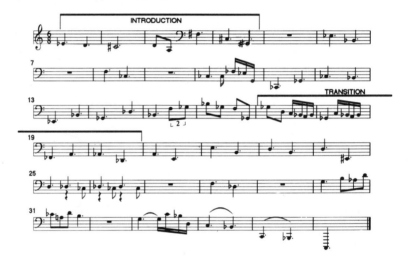

EXAMPLE 9-27. Skriabin: Op. 59 No. 2, reduction.

EXAMPLE 9-28. Skriabin: Op. 63 No. 2, reduction.

EXAMPLE 9-29. Lopatnikov: Sonatina Op. 7, first movement, bars 1–20.

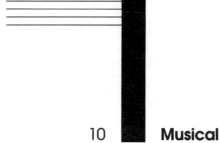

EXAMPLE 10-1. Lourié: *Syntheses* No. 1, bars 1–11.

EXAMPLE 10-2. Shillinger: "Heroic Poem" Op. 12 No. 1, bars 5–15.

EXAMPLE 10-3. Roslavets: Poem (1916), bars 22–35.

EX. 10-3. (cont.)

EXAMPLE 10-4. Obukhov: *Berceuse of a Blessed.*

a. bars 1–5.

b. bars 40–49.

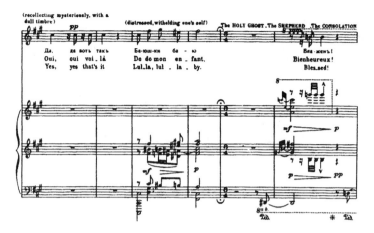

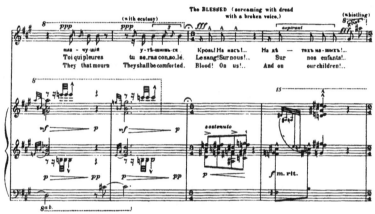

EXAMPLE 10-5. Prokofiev: *Visions fugitives* Op. 22 No. 5 (1915).

a. bars 1–7.

EX. 10-5b. bars 12–19.

EXAMPLE 10-6. Saminsky: Setting of "Song of Solomon" Op. 28 No. 4.

EXAMPLE 10-7. Saminsky: Setting of "Ah, This Misting Day" Op. 28 No. 6.

EXAMPLE 10-8. Saminsky: Setting of "Deli Yaman" Op. 28 No. 2.

a. bars 1-12.

b. bars 23-25.

EXAMPLE 10-9. Eikhgorn: Setting of "The Poor One."

EXAMPLE 10-10. Saminsky: Setting of "On the Distant Ridge" Op. 28 No. 3.

EXAMPLE 10-11. A. Tcherepnin: *Sunny Day* (1915), bars 1–13.

EXAMPLE 10-12. Prokofiev: *Visions fugitives*, Op. 22 No. 20 (1916).

a. bars 1–13.

b. bars 22–24.

EXAMPLE 10-13. A. Tcherepnin: *Pieces Without Title* No. 1, bars 1–13.

EX. 10-13 (cont.)

EXAMPLE 10-14. A. Tcherepnin: *Pieces Without Title* No. 2.

a. bars 1–10.

b. bars 28–32.

EXAMPLE 10-15. Prokofiev: *Visions fugitives* Op. 22 No. 10 (1915).

a. bars 1–6.

b. bars 13–16.

EXAMPLE 10-16. Prokofiev: *Visions fugitives* Op. 22 No. 13 (1916), bars 1–15.

EXAMPLE 10-17. Prokofiev: *Visions fugitives* Op. 22 No. 16 (1915).

a. bars 1–10.

EX. 10-17b. bars 27–34.

EXAMPLE 10-18. Mosolov: Sonata No. 2 Op. 4, first movement, bars 1–26.

EXAMPLE 10-19. Lourié: *Syntheses* No. 4.

a. bars 1–30.

EX. 10-19a (cont.)

b. reduction.

EX. 10-19b (cont.)

EXAMPLE 11-1. Skriabin: Prelude Op. 74 No. 2, bars 1–7.

a. score.

b. reduction.

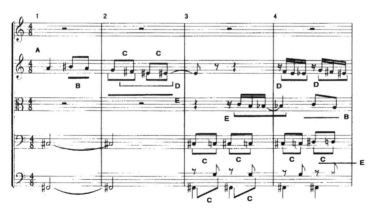

EX. 11-1b (cont.)

EXAMPLE 11-2. Mosolov: Sonata No. 1 Op. 3.

a. bars 1–8.

b. reduction.

EXAMPLE 11-3. Shostakovich: Sonata Op. 12, bars 1–5.

EXAMPLE 11-4. Skriabin: Prelude Op. 74 No. 4, reduction.

EXAMPLE 11-5. Lopatnikov: Sonatina Op. 7, third movement.

a. bars 1–15.

b. bars 56–67.

c. bars 96-108.

d. bars 126-48.

EXAMPLE 11-6. Skriabin: *Vers la flamme* Op. 72, reduction.

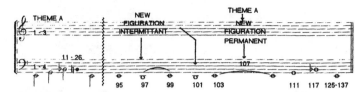

EXAMPLE 11-7. Sabaneyev: Sonata Op. 15, bars 308–13.

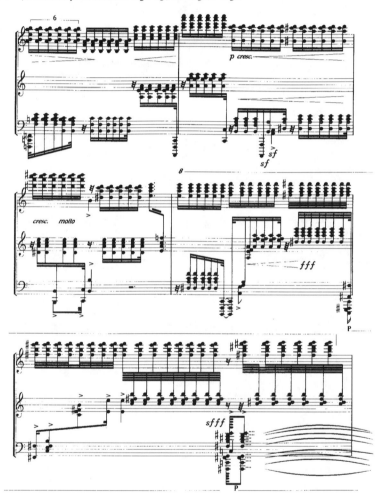

EXAMPLE 11-8. Lopatnikov: Sonatina Op. 7, first movement, bars 37–48.

EXAMPLE 11-9. Roslavets: Poem (1916), reduction.

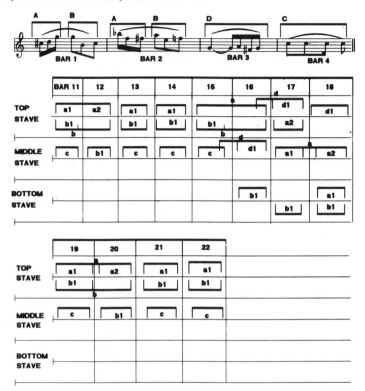

EXAMPLE 11-10. Lourié: Sonatina No. 3.

a. bars 1-10.

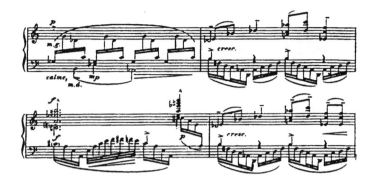

b. reduction.

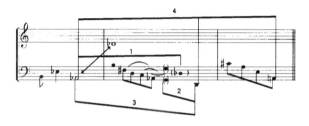

EXAMPLE 11-11. Lourié: *Syntheses* No. 3.

a. reduction.

b. reduction.

EX. 11-11c. bars 1–22.

EX. II-IIc (cont.)

EXAMPLE II-I2. Lourié: *Syntheses* No. 3, reduction.

EXAMPLE 11-13. Deshevov: *Meditations* Op. 3 No. 7.

EXAMPLE 11-14. Prokofiev: *Visions fugitives* Op. 22 No. 11.

a. bars 1–9.

b. bars 13–16.

EXAMPLE 11-15. B. Aleksandrov: Op. 1 Nos. 1 and 2 (1928), reduction.

EXAMPLE 11-16. B. Aleksandrov: Dance Op. 1 No. 1 (1928).

EX. II-16 (cont.)

EXAMPLE II-17. B. Aleksandrov: Scherzo Op. 1 No. 2.

Allegro Vivace (♩. = 160)

EX. 11-17 (cont.)

EXAMPLE 11-18. Lourié: *Syntheses* No. 1, reduction.

EXAMPLE 11-19. Lourié: *Forms in the Air.*

a. first movement, extracts.

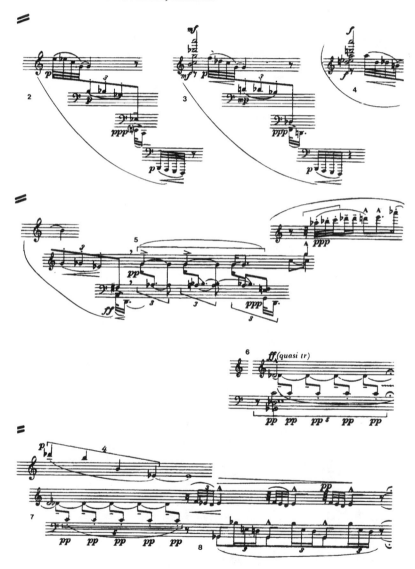

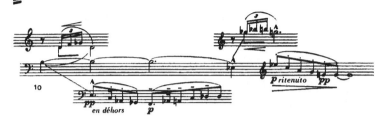

b. second movement, extracts.

EX. 11-19b (cont.)

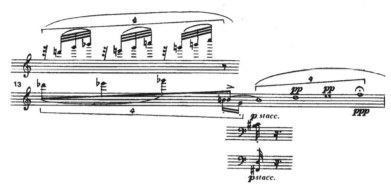

c. third movement, extracts.

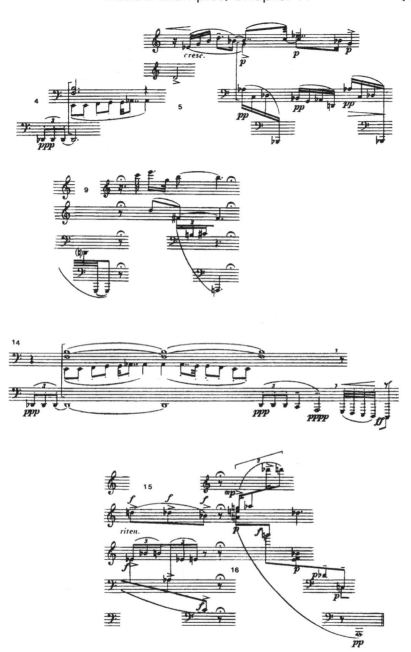

EX. 11-19d. reduction.

e. extracts.

f. scale.

EXAMPLE 12-1. A. Krein: Sonata Op. 34, reduction.

Bars Containing the Reference Chord

1,2	36,45	133,134					224	
Intro-duction 1–16 B	Exposi-tion 17–84 C♯–G	Middle Section B♭–B–F♯–C				Tran-sition 184–99	Recapi-tulation 200–53 C♯–G	Coda 254–66 B
	17–46 C♯–B						200–25 C♯–B	
	47–56 C♯/G						226–35	
	57–63					149–54	236–45	
						155–62 F♯ (C)	246–53 G (C♯)	
		85–90 B♭	105–10 C♯					
		91–97 A♭	111–17 B					
			118–27 G					
		98–104 B♭	128–32 B					254–66 B
1–5 B				133–38B				
6–16								
				139–48				
	64–84 C♯/G				163–83 C			
						184–99		

EXAMPLE 12-2. Mosolov: Sonata No. 2 Op. 4, first movement, reduction.

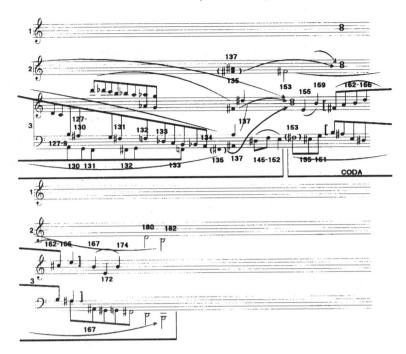

EXAMPLE 12-3. Mosolov: Sonata No. 2 Op. 4, first movement.

a. bars 109–18.

EX. 12-3b. bars 125–39.

c. bars 149–61.

EXAMPLE 12-4. Mosolov: Sonata No. 2 Op. 4, first movement, extracts.

EXAMPLE 12-5. Mosolov: Sonata No. 2 Op. 4, first movement, scale.

EXAMPLE 12-6. Skriabin: Sonata No. 10 Op. 70 (1913), reduction.

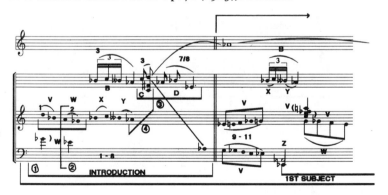

EX. 12-6 (cont.)

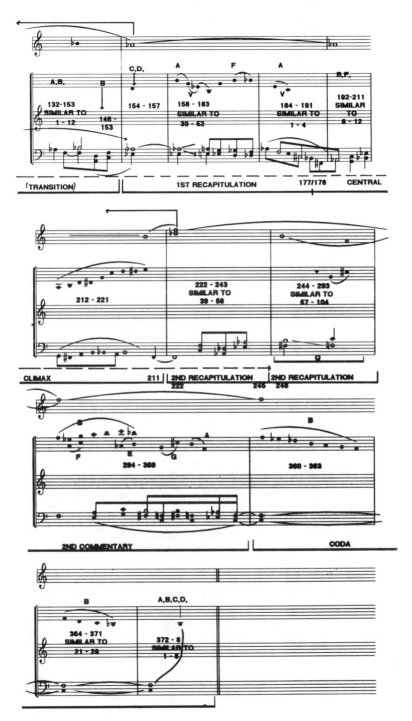

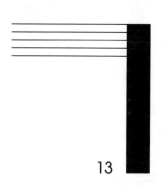

EXAMPLE 13-1. Ornstein: "Dwarfs at Dawn" Op. 11 No. 1.

EX. 13-1 (cont.)

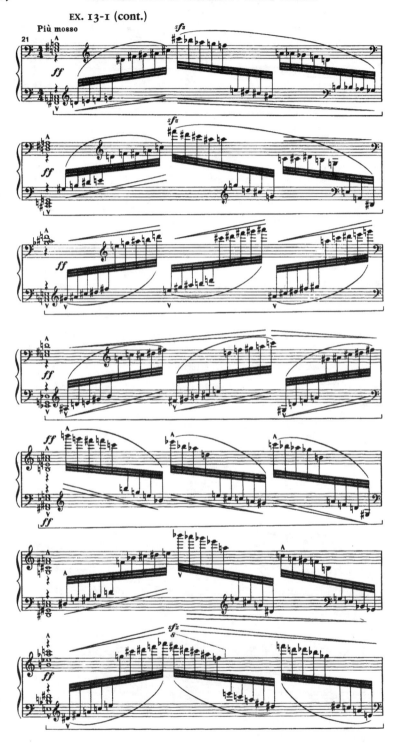

EX. 13-1 (cont.)

EXAMPLE 13-2. Ornstein: Prelude Op. 20 No. 1 (1914).

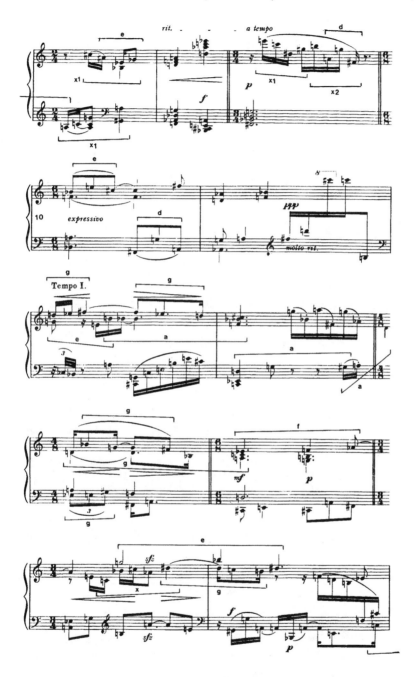

EX. 13-2 (cont.)

EXAMPLE 13-3. Ornstein: Prelude Op. 20 No. 2.

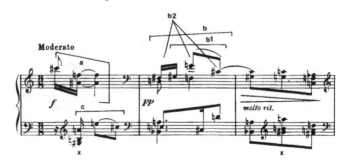

EX. 13-3 (cont.)

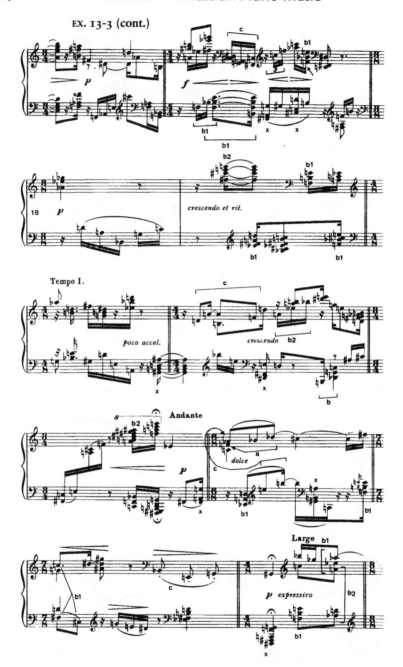

EXAMPLE 13-4. Roslavets: *Three Compositions* No. 1 (1914), reduction.

EXAMPLE 13-5. Roslavets: *Three Compositions* No. 2 (1914).

EXAMPLE 13-6. Roslavets: *Quasi Prelude* (1915).

EX. 13-6 (cont.)

EXAMPLE 13-7. Roslavets: *Quasi Prelude*, chart.

Bar and beat	Transposition of set	Bass note	Position of bass note in series	No. of pitches that move in and out at statement of set	
1a	TO	B♭	1	–	3
1b	5	A♯	5	3	2
2a	8	B♭	3	2	3
2b	3	D	2	3	2
2c	6	D♭	6	2	3
3a	11	E♭♭	4	3	2
3b	2	C♯	2	2	3
4a	7	D	6	3	2
4b	10	D♭	4	2	2
4c	1	F♭	4	2	3
5	5	E	2	3	3
6a	0	E♯	5	3	2
6b	3	F	3	2	3
6c–7	8	E♭	6	3	3
7a	0	D	3	3	3
7b	5	C♯	7	3	2
===					
8a	8	C♭	4	2	3
8b	1	C	2	3	2
8c	10	D♭	4	2	3
9a	3	D	2	3	2
9b	6	C♯	6	2	3
10a	11	D	4	3	2
10b	2	C	1	2	3
11a	9	C♯♯	5	3	2
11b	6	C♯	6	2	3
11c	1	E	4	3	2
12a	10	D♯	5	2	3
12b	3	D	2	3	3
13a	8	E♭	6	3	2
13b	5	E	2	2	2
13c	8	D♯♯	7	2	3
14a	1	D♯	3	3	2
14b	4	D♯	2	2	3
14c	9	C♯♯	5	3	3
15a	2	C	1	3	2
15b	5	C	6	2	3
16	10	D♭	4	3	2
17	1	C♭	1	2	3
18	6	D	7	3	3
19	11	D	4	3	2
20	2	C	1	2	3
21	7	B♯	5	3	3
===					

EX. 13-7 (cont.)

Bar and beat	Transposition of set	Bass note	Position of bass note in series	No. of pitches that move in and out at statement of set	
22a	0	G	6	3	3
22b	5	C	6	3	2
22c	8	E♭	6	2	3
22d	3	D	2	3	2
22e	6	D♭	6	2	3
23a	11	G♭	6	3	2
23b	2	A	6	2	3
24	7	D	6	3	3
25a	0	E♯	5	3	3
25b	8	C♭	4	3	3
26	3	B♭	6	3	2
27a	0	G	6	2	3
27b	7	D	6	3	3
27c	0	G	6	3	–

EXAMPLE 13-8. Roslavets: *Quasi Prelude*, transpositions of the set.

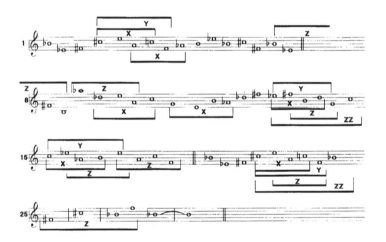

EXAMPLE 13-9. Roslavets: *Quasi Prelude*, reduction.

EXAMPLE 13-10. Roslavets: *Quasi Poem* (1915).

EX. 13-10 (cont.)

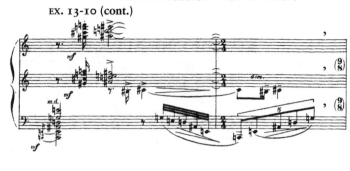

EX. 13-10 (cont.)

EXAMPLE 13-11. Roslavets: *Quasi Poem*, reduction.

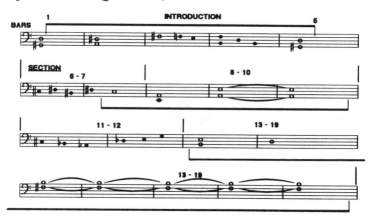

EXAMPLE 13-12. Roslavets: *Quasi Poem*, chart.

Bar and beat	Transposition of set	Bass note	Scale
	Introduction		
1	TO	G♯	A
1–3			Irregular
4a	3	B	A
4b	0	D	A
4c–5	0	C♭/G♯	B
	Section 1		
6a	0	C♯	C
6b	5	D♯	C
6c	0	B♯	D
7a	5	D♯	C
7b	0	B♯	D
7c	0	B♯	E
8a	0	E	F
8b	7	E	A+
9a	10	A	A+
9b–10	2	A	E
11a	6	C♯	C
11b	5	B♭	C
11c	0	A♭	G
12a	2	D♭	C

EX. 13-12 (cont.)

Bar and beat	Transposition of set	Bass note	Scale
12b	6	E	G
12c	9	F$\times$	A+
13		B	Irregular
14a		D	Irregular
14b	6	D	E
15a	2	F$\sharp$	F
15b	9	F$\sharp$	A+
16a		F$\sharp$	Irregular
16b–19	9	F$\sharp$	A+
	Interlude		
20–23			Irregular
	Section 2		
24a	1	A	A
24b	10	C	A
24c	10	,B$\flat\flat$	B
25a	10	F	A
25b	0	B$\flat\flat$	B
25c	10	E$\sharp$	A
26	9	A	B
27a	6	D	A
27b	11	C$\sharp$	A(−)
27c	1	C	B
28a	11	G	A(−)
28b	5	D$\flat$	B
28c	11	G	A(−)
29	1	C$\sharp$	B
30a	4	B$\sharp$	A
30b	1	D$\sharp$	A
30c	0	C	B
31a	1	G$\sharp$	A
31b	0	C	B
31c	1	G$\sharp$	A
32a	0	C	B
32b	1	G$\sharp$	A
32c	0	C	B
33–37	0	G$\sharp$/D	A+

EXAMPLE 13-13. Roslavets: *Quasi Poem*, scales.

EX. 13-13 (cont.)

EX. 13-13 (cont.)

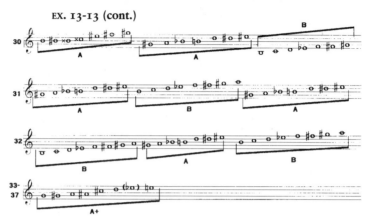

EXAMPLE 13-14. Golyshchev: Trio. (Open noteheads containing crosses are to be read as sharps.)

a. first movement, "Mezzo-Forte."

EX. 13-14a (cont.)

b. second movement, "Fortissimo," excerpts.

EX. 13-14c. third movement, "Piano," excerpts.

EX. 13-14d. fourth movement, "Pianissimo," excerpts.

Musical Examples, Chapter 14

EXAMPLE **14-1**. Bridge.

a. *Ecstasy.*

b. *Bittersweet.*

EXAMPLE 14-2. Ravel: String Quartet.

a. second movement, reduction.

b. first movement, reduction.

c. first movement, reduction.

EXAMPLE 14-3. Huré: La Cathédrale (1910–12), bars 40–44.

Index of Sources and Scores Consulted

I am indebted to the following libraries for the opportunity to study scores among their holdings. Numerals given after the name of a composition refer to these libraries; if no number is present, the score is in print.

Key to Library Codes

Aleksandrov, Anatoly. Sonata No. 3 Op. 18: 2, 24; Sonata No. 6 Op. 26: 2, 24

Aleksandrov, Boris. Dance and Scherzo Op. 1 (pub. 1928): 24

Bely. Sonatina Op. 5 (pub. 1929): 24

Deshevov. March Op. 1 No. 2 (pub. 1935): 2; *Meditations* Op. 3 (pub. ca. 1921): 32; Scherzo Op. 6 (1924): 24; Ballade Op. 7 (pub. 1927): 2, 32; *Rails* Op. 16: 6, 32

Feinberg. Sonata No. 1 Op. 1: 2; Sonata No. 2 Op. 2: 2, 4; Sonata No. 3 Op. 5: 2; Sonata No. 4 Op. 6 (1918): 7, 8; Fantasia No. 2 Op. 9 (1919): 0; Sonata No. 5 Op. 10 (1921): 2, 7, 8; Four Studies Op. 11 (pub. 1923): 7; Sonata No. 6 Op. 13 (1918): 2, 7, 8; Three Preludes Op. 15 (1922): 2, 7; *Humoresque* Op. 19 (pub. 1932): 0; Tchouvach Melodies Op. 24 No. 1: 0

Golyshchev. String Trio (ca. 1925): 29

Grechaninov. Songs Op. 47 (pub. 1911): 30; Songs (Baudelaire) Op. 48 (pub. 1911): 30; *Poème Dramatique* (Heine and Solovyev) Op. 51 (1910): 26; Four Mazurkas Op. 53 (pub. 1911): 36; *Pastels* Op. 61: 36

Krein, Aleksandr. Pieces Op. 18: 2, 7, 24; Pieces Op. 30: 2, 7, 24; Sonata Op. 34 (1922): 2, 7, 24

Krein, Grigory. Sonata Op. 27 (1925): 2, 7, 24

Kriukov. Sonata No. 2 Op. 14 (1922–24): 2; *Schlaflose Nacht* (Tiutschev) (1923): 8, 24

Index of Musical Examples

Examples identified by small roman numerals appear in the Notes of the chapters cited.

Gerard McBurney

London Jan 1996